I0136348

Living Love Letters Beyond Time and Space

Dr. Marc

Copyright © 2011 Dr. Marc

All rights reserved. No part of this book may be used or reproduced by any means, graphic, electronic, or mechanical, including photocopying, recording, taping or by any information storage retrieval system without the written permission of the publisher except in the case of brief quotations embodied in critical articles and reviews.

Balboa Press books may be ordered through booksellers or by contacting:

Balboa Press
A Division of Hay House
1663 Liberty Drive
Bloomington, IN 47403
www.balboapress.com
1-(877) 407-4847

Because of the dynamic nature of the Internet, any web addresses or links contained in this book may have changed since publication and may no longer be valid. The views expressed in this work are solely those of the author and do not necessarily reflect the views of the publisher, and the publisher hereby disclaims any responsibility for them.

ISBN: 978-1-4525-3278-3 (sc)

Any people depicted in stock imagery provided by Thinkstock are models, and such images are being used for illustrative purposes only. Certain stock imagery © Thinkstock.

Printed in the United States of America

Balboa Press rev. date: 2/11/2011

BALBOA
PRESS
A DIVISION OF HAY HOUSE

From 1961 to the Present

Insights along the Journey Inward … Coming Home!

There Is Love March 26, 1981

It Is in Loving that We LIVE …

And in Living that We LOVE …

Marc

1964: We are all searching for love, a world in search of love … Desperately looking and hoping to find it! 2005: Sadly we look outward … never looking inside. 2008: We are the love … you are the love … Be the LOVE!

Words are, at best, a poor excuse to express that which cannot be expressed. (1963)

Speak with the Smile, the Laugh and (Love with the Eyes*). (2010) Marc

*Twelfth Gyalwang Drukpa.

For my children, who believed totally in the Magic Butterfly, that they may come to dwell in their hearts, and experience a universal freedom that leads to a rich and fulfilling life.

For friends and strangers along the way, who have over the years asked if I could share these spontaneously arising expressions. To everyone who wants to believe in unconditional love, in self-realization, self-arising, self-loving, overflowing onto all and everything … love.

The Journey Inward

HEART—You can't get Here From There—MIND

A BUTTERFLY … Ah … Now that's Better!

Aha … SMILE … Even Better!

And so It Begins

The Beginning (I Wake Up!) 1961–1963

A View from the Street

I walk across a barren land, seen differently by others …

To me …
A huge windswept dessert … Hunger scrawled on the masses' face,
The cripple limping aimlessly …

Who is so secure as not to see … a ragged child coveting candy?

How can they see gardens and trees where in reality exists deserts … dried up seas?

November 2, 2002

An open letter to my friends and loved ones: If we live today with LOVE, tomorrow is filled with limitless possibilities for Hope and Peace. Let's rediscover the love within ourselves, and reach out with it.

1963–1968

I, who Love myself, LOVE You, Who Loves yourself, Who Loves me, who loves myself, Who LOVES YOU, WHO LOVES ME, WHO LOVE YOURSELF (A. Ginsberg) and (also me, Jesus, and Buddha and so on …).

April 1971

To Whom It May Concern

When did you last feel the rain,
Were caressed by the wind,
Or pondered others' pain?

So insecure within, unable to reach out,
Cherishing masochistic dreams, destroying others with your doubts …

Crying about insincerity, while sifting pebbles through your hands,
And when did you last … really give a Damn?

(We are overly self-sensitive, yet insensitive to the sensitiveness of others.)

July 1977

Pediatric Oncology Rotation

Tiny Little Hand

You looked into me, too young, too old …

Through the silent night, your tiny hand to hold …

I too naïve to see your wings unfold …

Your only wish, to have a hand to hold …

My eyes, heavy laden with sleep, did not take note, as your spirit soared beyond my grasp, little hand free at last …

(We are all interdependent!)

And I WAKE UP … Again! 1970s through 1980s

Harmony's Discord

The muted tones of Life around me injure my ears, as this out-of-tune piano plays—
Ludwig gone deaf, Schubert unfinished—

My soul burning, ignited by the chorus growing brighter—

Cruel be the reality, pounding upon the piano's keyboard—

The soprano drowned out by the finale's dominant cord—

We are all real once more …

(Too often, all we see is our own projection … never really seeing the other … forever lost in a movie of our own delusion, sometimes nice, but still an illusion. That is why we can be "madly" in LOVE in one instance and in the next, "madly" in HATE with the once absolute object of our "LOVE" … LOVE—HATE.)

(NOT LOVE At ALL! So, first learn to Be Alone! Then,
Be Alone with oneself, go inside, get REAL, and then BE … Be the Love.)

Secret: You are the LOVE.

All Is Impermanent (but We Return Again and Again …).

Within, our Hearts Beat, the Rhythm of Life—

Between the space of Light and Dark,

We Live and Die and Live again—

The Ebb and Flow of the undulating Tide—
Footsteps, grains of sand, autumn leaves, whispers on the wind …

Illusory … 1970

(Relax … don't rush … patience … slow down. We are not leaving this life alive, so Be Here and Now … in the ever-present … precious transitory life.)

LAMENT (February 7, 1988) At a bedside in the ICU

The Flame of your Life extinguished in a moment—

You left this world so quickly, while friends and loved ones waited with Hope—

Life impermanent, illusory; we are here but for the Moment, and the Moment is gone.

A Close Encounter with LOVE's Awareness (February 23, 1988)

You were there but for a moment, and for a moment I was alive—

In the flickering of a candle's flame, life begins and ends, to begin again—

I held the Dove in my hand, feeling its warmth, Heart fluttering—

Fingers outstretched … Fly—

My longing shattered by your beauty in flight—

Hope Eternal, my Love.

(Love can only be held in the outstretched palm … in the clenched fist it Dies.)*

*OSHO

A Lover's Prayer (January 25, 1988—a prior remembering)

I met you somewhere, in some enchanted place, in some corner of my mind,
When my soul was forlorn but my tiny heart open—

I know we will recognize each other; we will meet in some unexpected place;
Your face will stand out—

I scan the crowded streets, you are in the markets, and You are there—

My heart feels your warmth, your tenderness, your soul—

As I sit in front of the fire's flame, I bask in your glow—

You are there … I know.

(Trust in Existence; The Universe knows what it is doing* … we have been together before [2005]).

*Twelfth Gyalwang Drukpa.

AWARENESS (March 17, 1981)

To TOUCH … a winged bird in flight—

To FEEL … the caress of the ebb tide—

The SUN'S Rays dancing upon the water before vanishing from sight—

The MOON ever present, saving us from night—

As the DOVE fell from the sky for a brief second, before touching Earth resuming flight—

For a PRECIOUS MOMENT, I held LIFE.

Yesterday's Steps (March 14, 1981)

A Woman-Child, You filled my soul—

Restored me to myself, having made me whole—

Yesterday's steps are really never gone—

Traveling through my past toward a new dawn—

I am once more,

Once more reborn …

We are born with a collective awareness … trust that within you is an ageless, timeless knowledge … the inner wisdom … you have been here before … Now Be … Here, Now … go inside and reconnect with your truth … you are not your name … not your parents or your job, but so much more … ageless and timeless … perfect.

For I Had Yet to Know (Tiny Little Hand Remembered)

You look at me and Know—

As the seconds tick in the stillness of the night, your outstretched hand holds me tight—

I am drawn to your eyes, all-knowing, your face, a woman-child suspended in time, tiny little hand in mine—

Four years, yet a Sage. How? Why? Not mine to understand; it is for me to simply hold this precious little hand—

As I keep sentry by your side, my hand unfolds; sleep overcomes even the strongest of souls—

I awake to the early morning light, the sun's rays dancing, but you have journeyed out of sight—

I rage against the dying of the light … for I have yet to know, and you have Journeys yet to go … (October 19, 2002).

Spontaneous Meditation (October 2002)

While sitting in a new yet familiar space, focused on a Photo,* knowing a future meeting will take place—

A loud knock, you burst in, I glimpse your face, my gaze doesn't shift, in meditation—

A spontaneous trust and a relaxation—

In my inner silence I recognize you, be assured I am here for you, I have always been here for you and you for I—

Long ago I held your hand in another place and time—

We meet and meet and dance and dance in this world and the next—

Forever have you been and will always be … one heart … connection …

(And so it again happens, mutual recognition, a challenge to loose the self and see the other and experience loving compassion.) Dropping the Mind … going beyond Time and Space …

*Shortly thereafter, I was introduced to the twelfth Gyalwang Drukpa, whose photo had put me in spontaneous meditation. I had never heard of him in this lifetime, nor did I mention this experience to anyone. That meeting significantly enhanced my life! I also became aware of a singularly remarkable woman … Back on the Path!

Don't Be Too Serious (October 2002)

I saw your tears in the rain, reflecting children's laughter in a puddle.

The Challenge is to know that the inner child of absolute Wisdom and Unconditional Acceptance, exists as IT ... has always been, and to remain childlike in your experience of all you encounter ... then can you Be ... present in all things ... Relaxed and Free, nonjudgemental, all knowing ... and Trusting of Yourself ... No Questions ... or Problems no longer obstacles but opportunities for Creativity, resulting in solutions ... Every moment an Awakening, until all separation dissolves and oneness remains ... interdependency of all and everything ... the universe now experienced within ... ever expanding ... limitless ... embracing all!

DEAR and Glorious EXISTENCE (to baba-au-rhumba@)

Beloved, Trust This, that we will drop the past and even now as we have experienced such beautiful moments, spaces, infinities of freedom, free expressions without fear … in the successive moments all will be more and the never-ending beauty unfolding within, we shall share with the other as a bountiful harvest of God, of life of love of peace of hope … a doorway unto thee that cannot close, for once opened is light eternal. I feel you now and always, my life, my love, my heart. May we always be a door unto the other, a bed for the other to rest upon. A Lamp … the Light of Truth unto where no darkness can come, that we may never stray from the truth, forever in the present, forever in life and in that which we know to lay beyond … in this world but not of it!

We walk side by side, respectful of the other by taking care of the self! Characterless and forever grateful for the knowledge that has been shared as we cradle it as a newborn child pure from our very hearts and souls! Our Hearts are now open, and LOVE overflows onto all and everything, LIFE DIVINE … (December 18, 2004).

Letters to Baba au Rhumba (AWAKENED!)

A Wake-Up Call (a time of connecting with Fully Realized Beings),

A time of challenging Love, of Loving challenges and beginning the Journey Inward.

On the Journey Inward and with Trust, a Heart Connection with the other arises, and Awareness starts to come to the surface. I expressed them in a series of letters to my Beloved Friend titled, "Letters to Baba au Rhumba." I laugh, as that Baba au Rhum was her favorite dish (2004 through 2008).

Loves challenge and Reward is to drop our projection, our story and see the Other!

Become a highly polished mirror of consciousness, Reflecting the Other.

The Most Serious Business in the Universe: CHILDREN at PLAY!

As we skip along, Friends with no mind, Children with no sense of time … Wandering, humming, skipping, dancing, jumping, rolling, climbing, falling—

Always LAUGHING … discovering in every moment some great new Wonder … Ah, a grasshopper with a rainbow color: have you ever seen such a wonder? … Next, a blade of grass like no other … forever Wonder … forever JOY! WaLah! Whatever … No Matter … No Past … No Future in the Here and Now … the entire splendor of the Universe within the grasp of our tiny hands right here in our backyard sandbox and all … Precious Friend, All Children Know This and That … Inner Freedom Rings in every Song this Message Sings, I Who LOVE Myself, LOVES YOU who LOVE Yourself!

Playmates Always, Lovers Never, Friends Forever … (October 15, 2005).

TRUST THIS! TRUST YOURSELF! YOUR INNER WISDOM!

In our union of the Self-less, we have approached through the other that which mirrors the hope of the Divine … it is in that realization We ARE AWARE, One Love, One Heart, into the Light of Infinite Emptiness … Precious Total TRUST … the Abundance of the HEART … now Compassion Overflows! (October 10, 2005)

THE MIND IS A TOMBSTONE!

(This awareness is of you and through you and with you, and I Thank You.)

The MIND is a TOMBSTONE carved in GRANITE by someone other than YOU! That which we have been taught to value, so-called knowledge, Really nothing more than a DEAD PAST. A goblet within which to hold FEAR and Foster a False Sense of NEED, DESIRE, PERSONALITY, EGO, SUFFERING all Fabrications of the MIND: A Cultural Prison to Enslave and Control! True Knowledge can only be Experienced! To recognize this Fabrication of the Mind is in a split second to Shatter that Tomb and step into the LIGHT … to reclaim your God-given Birthright … forever FREE, forever CONSCIOUS, forever SELF-LOVING, RELAXED-FLOWING-EVERPRESENT. The Mind is DEAD Intellectualism; INTELLEGENCE is LIVING-BREATHING-always CHANGING, Always NEW … FLOWING only and always in the PRESENT!!! (October 23, 2005)

LIFE IS REAL ONLY THEN WHEN I AM* … (After reading Gurdjieff*)

I am Real only when I am flowing with Existence … in the center is a total RELATEDNESS … in the EVER-PRESENT NOW … at the CENTER of ALL and EVERYTHING … The ENDLESS RESEVOIR of the CENTER. This is CREATIVITY and TRUTH … Always at the Center! To enter the MIND is to Leave the Center … to leave the Body and enter the Ego … to Abandon your Heart and embrace the Personality … EGO where all is Illusory yet perceived as reality … to FALL from the FLOW of that which is eternal, ONLY through this REALIZATION can we drop back in to the Body and BE Real, Ever present, in TRUTH. AWARENESS. Our Relatedness can only Be EXPERIENCED in the presence of TRUTH and EXISTENCE, which are inseparable! REALIZED only in the TOTALITY of the BODY … Drop the Mind … Enter the Body … Experience the One HEART … feel all and everything interconnected … FREEDOM! (I know you know this and that, said the Cat in the Hat … Major Tom, Captain Jack … over and out) (October 28, 2005)

GoD-Ess! TRUTH

Jesus Loved Mary beyond Explanation, He Honored Her for Her Purity of HEART—

She was wholehearted. They related with total Trust. For he recognized that she is Goddess, as is the potential of all women!

Together, a Balance was achieved that to this day threatens the status quo of Roman-Dominated Civilization.

The Awareness that …

War, Greed, Jealousy, and most importantly, that Enslavement in all of its forms are impossible when the REALIZATION of that COMPASSION is present in us all …

Mary of Magdala is all women … the awareness of this truth by women will free them to be WOMEN once more (October 2005).

Favorite Smoothie Recipe (A Love Letter)

Hi Sunflower (seedling): I am sharing this with you as we might share our favorite dessert; berries, cream, abundance! Mmmmmm, Yummy! (We have many favorites!)

Often one might return kindness with kindness or feel a pleasant warmth from one so kind; when we receive gracious support so do we want to express heartfelt appreciation. LOVE knows nothing of these things! Nor does LOVE need them! For LOVE is an arrow, straight and true … directed from the Divine, piercing the Heart and connecting the souls of the intended Lovers through the Other … through and through with the Divine! To SURRENDER to this total TRUTH is to LIBERATE the SOUL and unite with the DIVINE … forever AWARE! (I believe this is a shared awareness between us) A Delicious Nourishing Smoothie of DIVINE LOVE … a Gift of the UNIVERSE!! Dear Heart: if this feels good, Sip On, if not, RELAX, as it is just a smoothie mixed with Love … (December 2005).

(Through the Other we Experience the self on a Journey that leads to Awareness and realization and freedom … ever onward … ever inward … to look into the Mirror … and to see our reflection … and to then go beyond it … to the Universal Truth … to the One Heart … The One LOVE … until our story is no more and we become all at once, One with all, the interconnectedness-interrelatedness that is the Universe, from where we came and where we are, self-acceptance … oneness … total relaxation in all things … Overflowing Love.)

THE GIFT

BELOVED SUNFLOWER SEED: DEATH comes to each and every one of us every day! This is our Liberation, and through this awareness, we have the power of conscious REBIRTH into the EVER-PRESENT, PRECIOUS GIFT, DIVINE LIFE. Always New, Always Flowing, Ever Changing, Ever Present in the HERE and NOW! The AWE and SPLENDOR of the UNIVERSE is CONTAINED within EACH and EVERY ONE of US!

We are the Unlimited potential of Creation! HOPE Everlasting … His Love DIVINE … The Gift to ALL BEINGS, active consciousness in each and every moment! THE DIVINE RELEASE, THE LETTING GO, THE COSMIC LEAP INTO THE LIMITLESS INNER UNIVERSE of the ONE TRUE HEART. COMPASSION without limits, FREE FLIGHT, the Seamless integration of Eagle and DOVE … This IS the LOVE that WE SHARE … May WE ALL Have The REALIZATION! EXISTENCE is taking CARE! LIVE … LOVE … LAUGH … CELEBRATE … TAKE CARE … YOU are PRECIOUS and PERFECT as are WE ALL (October 2005).

LET US DANCE

Let us Dance a more Loving Dance, born of the Love from the FULLNESS of EXPERIENCE that is Truly Unconditional! Without Expectations or Demands … Our True Nature … HEART to HEART! … DEAR HEART … BELOVED HEART (September 6, 2005).

OCEANIC VIBRATIONS

It is good to be in the truth with oneself, even though it may be unsettling at times to confront the self!

To surrender to existence is the only path, and with that, all is relaxed and easy!

I am Smiling and Laughing … inner Sunshine everywhere … LIFE IS BEAUTIFUL!

LOVE DIES in the presence of ATTACHMENT and then only Attachment remains … release attachment … float on the waves … Relax … Embrace!

In the presence of Attachment, all is FEAR … Choose Life over Death, let go, Release Attachment … float on the Waves … Relax and Embrace LOVE … It will direct you and release you … Its form will change, but its love always remains! Now BE … Be Free! TRUST YOURSELF … YOU KNOW THE TRUTH! YOU ARE OK!

A Nothing Nothings Nothing … Something!

In the Unknowing, in the Emptiness, all and everything is one. No pain, no need for freedom from pain. No LOVE, no HATE, no DESIRE, no JEALOUSY, no SEPARATION, no KNOWING. UNKNOWINGNESS is the CHILDLIKE state of Absolute Realness. TRUTH, direct connectedness to the universe, at one at once with all and everything! Only in Unknowing can we be free of our separate Delusionary personal Reality. We are not apart from the whole of existence! Only with that awareness can Existence Enter.

Then All is LOVE (January 8, 2006).

I LOVINGLY SHARE WITH YOU

What the Buddhists have always known (and what some Quantum Physicists, Cosmologists, and Astronomers may know), I lovingly share with you, BELOVED!

The Universe continuously recirculates, pulsating (the hallmark of life), Vibrating from Higher to lower then recirculating back toward the center in a higher vibration, a continuous wave … it's Alive! The Beginningless … Endless Universe … LIFE!

Matter is SENTIENT, and All Matter is Energy! (Alternating between Form and Formlessness! No-Thingness … in a continuous Vibration … the essence of all … Perpetual!).

TIME + SPACE = 0. Thus, everything is always in the Present! There is no separation between the Observer and the Observed. All events are not outside of us but One within us. The Observer is one with the Observed, Zero separation, thus you are always One with the Universe, as there is no separation! The Universe is all at one and at once within you.

The present is always! All there ever is, is the PRESENT! All is in the Present. See and then you know, the present is constant, there is nothing else, no division, no separation, just present!

All Habitats are temporary within the Universe, including the planet Earth! Formlessness is the basic nature of energy, neither can it be created nor destroyed, but merely Transformed! All is FORMLESS and SENTIENT! Hahahahaha … Skipping, Dancing, Laughing, Celebrating, Singing, Rope Walking, Fun Loving, Free, and Happy, in Love with LOVING, All is Always Here and NOW, so Drop In and Drop Out! ENJOY!

Ps. I Love You … (June 27, 2008).

Thank You: A Collection of Insights (for lack of a better description)

BELOVED, LOVED—

Be Loved, Be—

Always you are Beloved to me ... (April 7, 2006).

LOVE'S GIFT (2006)

I flow into you as naturally as a River flows into the Ocean,

Thank you for receiving me, Beloved ...

Greatest WISH! (2006)

My greatest wish is (we Be at Ease … with each other, ourselves and all things), a Joyous Dance, an unseen reflection, No self, a meditative life, "Love Loves Love!" (We each Be the Love).

Preciousness! (2006)

We are all one precious atom of existence—

A collective smile—

Life's Brilliance, a Celebration, a Rebirth … to be at ease, no more, no less, just that!

TRUTH

Truth simply is ... it needs nothing ... Not even a witness! When spoken, it is recognized by all ... (without explanation) (2006).

TIMELESS

I Linger by your side,

As a child by a babbling brook,

Enjoying the splendor of all your surprises—

No need, No want, No desire—

Just pure joy, Love for its own sake—

And nothing more ...

YOU ART THOU, and I AM THEE

Two centered souls, Children at play—

Serious work, Child's play!

Born again this very Day ... (December 8, 2006).

BLISS!/MANDALA

SHE INVITES ME ... to enter the Mandala between her Thighs—

SHE MAKES LOVE to ME with her Eyes—

A WHOLEHEARTED INVITATION—

A DIVINE INITIATION—

OUR BLISSFUL MEDITATION—

WE BOTH AWAKEN ... EYES OPEN WIDE ...

AS SPOKEN TO YOU … (June 28, 2006)

I am water, you can relax into me, surrender now, drop your mind, relax your body—

Float ON … IN ME—

I will wash over you in gentle waves, Relax … relax … I am washing over you—

You will not be lost … I am not here; all mind is illusion—

The core of you is resurrected NOW!

Nothing to be lost or found—

You ARE, as I Am … NO-THING—

PRECIOUS SOUL—

RELAX … AH … Om … and then the soul was Realized!

A FACT …

NEED can never be satisfied—

LOVE needs nothing; it is complete with in itself!

LOVE …

SADNESS comes, and sadness goes,

But LOVE Grows and GROWS …

FEAR

We are Born into Fear—

We are Nursed on Fear—

And we Breed Fear … We Must Change … Recognize the MIND is the source of FEAR—

The HEART knows no FEAR … ONLY LOVE … The HEART is FEARLESS—

Know this … enter your heart … drop your mind and be FEARLESS, LOVE!

(This Transformation into the HEART is the JOURNEY, the Path, the Light, the Way, Beyond the Mind, Beyond Fear …into the arms of LOVE!)

"LOVE Has Already WON."*

*Elisabeth.

"All and EVERYTHING"—is already here within us:

CONFUSION: Everyone is "Out" looking for love, acceptance, Look within, be self-accepting, realize you are the Love (for which you are looking).

WORDS: are, at best, a poor excuse to express that which cannot be expressed!

TRUTH: All is in the silence between the words, Feel the Breath as that carries the message, the heartbeat, the eyes, the smile … That is where all is spoken in silence, Heart to Heart.

BODY: a shrine, a home, a vehicle, your greatest lover, sacrificing for you in every moment, responding to your every wish and command, even unto its death. Never complaining, always loving you and never resting, that your spirit may.. Absolute perfection, a greater love has never been known by you. Take care to nurture your body; it is your greatest treasure! A Divine Mystery …

FAITH (December 23, 2007)

For those who can SEE, they will see the TRUTH …

For those who can HEAR, they will hear the TRUTH …

For those who can UNDERSTAND, they will understand the TRUTH …

For those among us who BECOME:

Mindless

Selfless

Emptiness

No-Thingness

LOVING without condition or expectation … TRUSTING …

THEY ARE THE TRUTH!

AN EXPLANATION

DEATH is the only constant … from the moment of physical Birth, it is only cellular of mind and body—

FEAR … All Fear is a fear of Death, nothing more—

DISTRUST … is a product of the Mind and Ego—

TRUTH is the ENERGY … the Prana, the BREATH … and is always Transcendent, Transformational, Never Dies—

ENERGY … is not of the Body … it is Eternal, Infinite, Renewable—

SUFFERING … We suffer because we are so intimate with our minds and our bodies!

YOU … are not your mind, and you are not your Body. This awareness is Meditation, the only way to TRANSCEND to the Energy—

PRESENT … FREE … LOVING!

ONLY THE HEART CAN EXPERIENCE THE TRUTH … THE ESSENCE of ALL THINGS … The ULTIMATE FLOWERING—NEVER ENDING …

LOVE: A Self-Arising Letter (August 5, 2010)

LOVE is effortless. Self-arising … as a River flowing freely from a Rock. It simply is, and no amount of effort can create it in its absence … But when present, no amount of effort can deny it! Neither can LOVE be Created or Destroyed, for all its Power it simply is (and when we embrace it … so simply are we, one).

When nurtured by a Heart connection, LOVE is Transformational. No power can persuade it, and no force can oppose it. All pursuits pale in its presence, and all material goals dissolve in its Manifestation.

LOVE has only one source and only one purpose … It is in and of the HEART and given freely to us as a GIFT of Divine COMPASSION … That we may know … the DIVINE in every moment and in all things and in each other.

Rejoice in LOVE … It is the GIFT that has been GIVEN Effortlessly and Undeniably!

The Beginning......................................Marc

www.ingramcontent.com/pod-product-compliance
Lightning Source LLC
Chambersburg PA
CBHW061354090426
42739CB00002B/27